Lene

24
Snowflakes
in Tatting

Akacia

Forlaget Akacia
Skovvænget 1
DK - 5690 Tommerup
akacia@akacia.dk

1. print, 2002
6. print, 2012
Printed at Dardedze Holografija, Riga

ISBN: 978-87-7847-052-2

Introduction

At the annual lace fair in Slagelse i Denmark it has become a tradition to decorate a Christmas tree and in 2001 The Danish Tatting Association (Dansk Orkisforening) was asked to decorate the tree.

There simply has to be snowflakes on a Christmas tree and there are no limits for creating them. I started out with just a few snowflakes in tatting just for a presentation, but then my creative mind got the better of me and the ideas started flowing. One snowflake took the other and suddenly I had 24 snowflakes - one for each day in December until Christmas. The snowflake for the twentyfourth day of December I decorated with glass beads and this created the real Christmas spirit!

Only the special tatting techniques used for the snowflakes are described in this book. A diagram as well as a brief description is included for all of the designs.

Happy tatting!

Lene Bjørn

Explanation of symbols

Chain

Ring

Picot = p

Split ring

Glass bead

Josephine knot = half knots formed into a ring

Spiral cord = half knots formed into a chain

Double knots = dk

Half double knots = hk

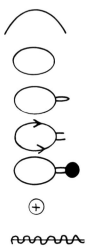

Materials

Shuttles
Crochet hook
Paper clips
A pair of scissors
Sewing needle
Glass beads
Starch
Crochet thread. All designs in this book are made up in AIDA no. 20 but any firm and smooth thread can be used.

Lock stitch and false picot

A lock stitch is made of a reversed 1st half of the stitch followed by a correct 2nd half of the stitch.
A false picot is created when you omit to tighten the 1st half of the stitch completely.

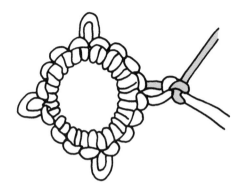

Glass beads = ●

How to crochet a glass bead onto a work.
Pull the thread through the pearl with a fine crochet hook or a thread, pass the shuttle through the loop and tighten it as an ordinary joining.

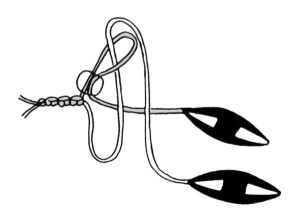

Ring on ring

Start the first ring like a chain but remember to leave a loop.

The second ring is tatted with the shuttle which created the knots for the first ring. Pull the ring together.

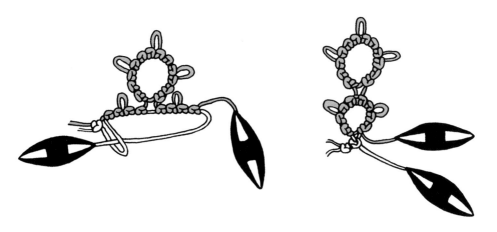

Finish tatting the first ring (as a chain).
Pass the shuttle through the loop and pull the first ring together.

Chain on chain

Tatted in two different ways.

First method: 2 shuttles.
Start with a paper clip, 6 dk, join together. *Turn and change shuttles, 1 dk, 1 small picot, 6 dk, join together*. Repeat from * to * as many times as shown in the pattern.

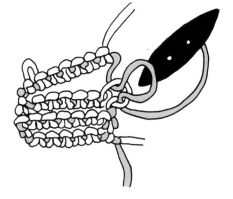

Second method: 1 shuttle + a ball thread.
Start with a paper clip, 6 dk, turn, 1 lock stitch (see page 5), 1 small picot, 6 dk, join together. *Turn, 1 lock stitch, 1 small picot, 6 dk, join together.* Repeat from * to *.

Remember! The closest shuttle thread is pulled through the loop you have created.

False chain

Left knot:

Join the shuttle thread down where the chain
has to end, the thread must be the same length
as the other chains.

Pull the shuttle thread under the chain thread
and upwards.

Pass the shuttle through the loop from behind -
from right towards left.
Pull the knot loosely.
Turn the knot under the chain thread and leave the
shuttle thread under the chain thread.

Right knot:

Pass the shuttle from forward and down through
the loop - from left towards right.

The thread is pulled tight = 1 dk.

The First Day of December

The snowflake is made in 2 rounds
or with 2 shuttles if you will tat with
split rings.

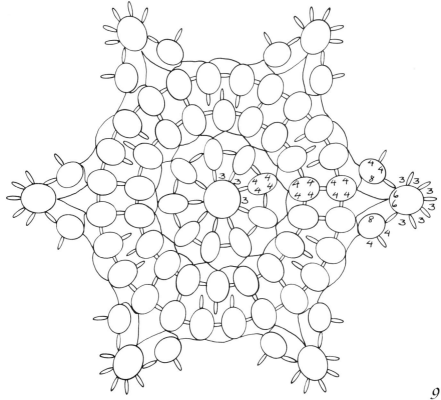

The Second Day of December

1 shuttle + a ball thread.
The snowflake is made in 2 rounds.
There are 3 dk between each picot.
First tat the middle and then the
outer round.
This snowflake can also be made
continuously with 2 shuttles according to the diagram.
Tat as usual until chain 12 where the
arrows point towards ring 14, join
the shuttle thread down at ring 1 and
tat chain 13 backwards, as illustrated
on page 8.

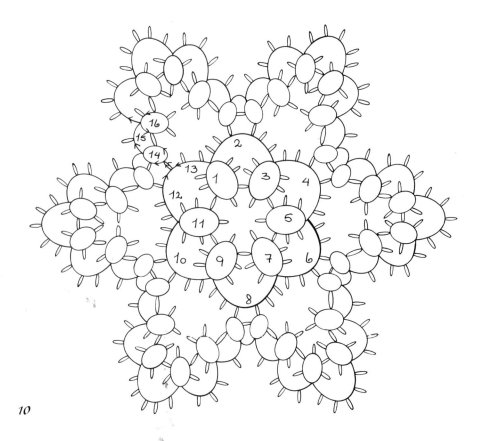

The Third Day of December

2 shuttles.

The snowflake is made in 7 rounds continuously.

Start with the inner ring with 3 dk between each picot, make a false picot towards round one. Each chain starts with a false picot and continues with 3 dk, 1 dk between each picot and is concluded with 3 dk.

All of the decorative picots should be long.

The Fourth Day of December

2 shuttles.
The snowflake is made in 2 rounds continuously.
There are 6 dk between each picot, but the outer ring have 3 dk between each picot.

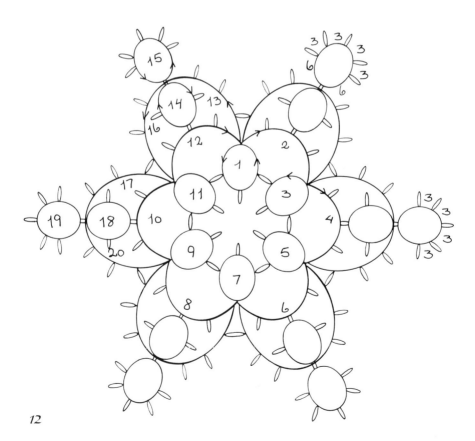

The Fifth Day of December

1 shuttle + a ball thread.
The snowflake is made in 3 rounds,
but do not cut the thread between
the rounds.
Round 1: start with a ring and then
a chain.
Round 2: only chains.
Round 3: chains and rings according
to the diagram.

The Sixth Day of December

2 shuttles.

The snowflake is made in 2 rounds according to the diagram.

Round 1: rings and chains.

Round 2: rings and chains, but at the joins change the shuttles to turn the chain the right way.

This snowflake can also be made continuously by making a false chain (see page 5) at the last chain in the first round.

14

The Seventh Day of December

2 shuttles.
The snowflake is made in 2 rounds
according to the diagram.

The Eighth Day of December

1 shuttle + a ball thread.
The snowflake is made in 2 rounds continuously.
Put a paper clip on the thread and then start the chain with 7 dk. After this the inner ring is tatted with 5 dk between the picots (5 p and 1 false picot). Each chain begins with 1 reversed 1st half of the stitch then the correct 2nd half of the stitch (illustrated on page 7 at the bottom), then 1 small p and 7 dk, join the shuttle thread to the previous small picot, and so on.

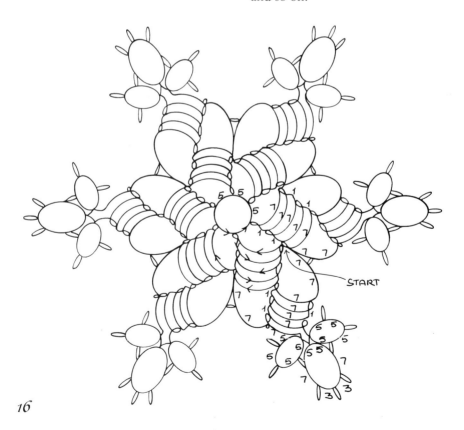

The Ninth Day of December

2 shuttles.

The snowflake is made in 1 round. Start the first chain with a paper clip, tat 8 dk, exchange shuttles and tat the inner ring. The chain is completed with 8 dk, 1 small p and 8 dk. Exchange shuttles and put on a paper clip again before making 1 dk, 1 small p and 8 dk, join to the first small picot, turn and exchange shuttles, and so forth.

Changing shuttles at each turn can be omitted by making a reversed right knot and a correct left knot (= 1 dk) before the small picot (see page 7 at the bottom).

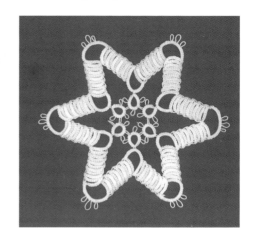

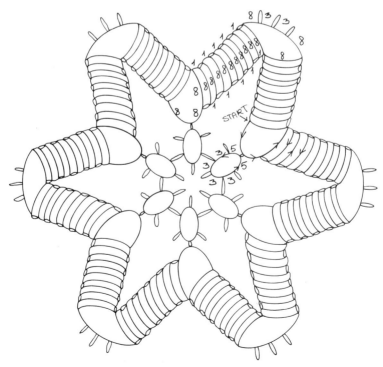

The Tenth Day of December

2 shuttles.

The snowflake is made in 2 rounds.

Round 1: start at ring A. The rings F and G are made as split rings.

Round 2: made up of rings and chains according to the diagram.

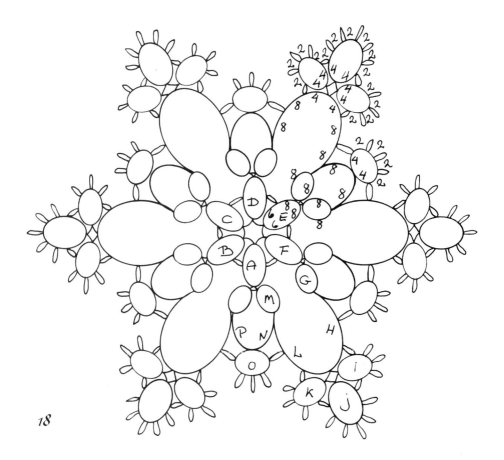

The Eleventh Day of December

2 shuttles.

The snowflake is made in 2 rounds.

There are 5 dk between each picot.

Round 1: start at ring A. The rings F and G are made as split rings.

Round 2: made up of rings and chains according to the diagram.

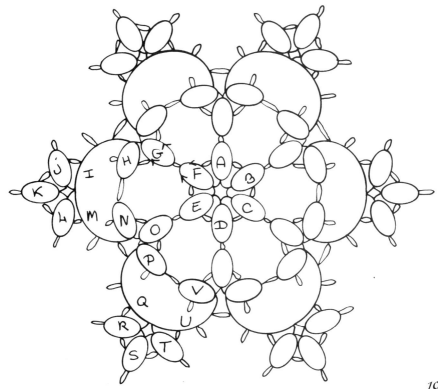

The Twelfth Day of December

2 shuttles.
The snowflake is made in 5 rounds according to the diagram. The ring F is a split ring. Start each chain with a small picot.

The Thirteenth Day of December

1 shuttle + a ball thread.
The snowflake is made in 5 rounds according to the diagram. The last picot in ring A is made as a false picot. Tat the chains B, C, D, E, F. The chain G is tatted until the last picot, then you join to the last picot in ring A and complete the chain G with a false chain (see page 8).

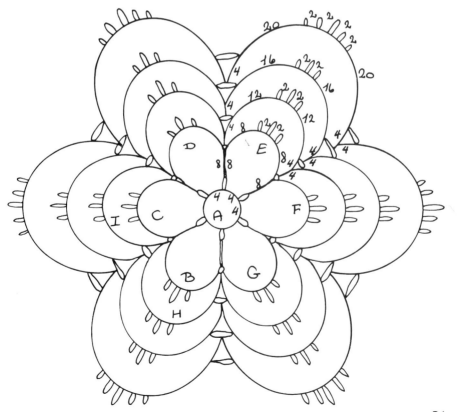

The Fourteenth Day of December

2 shuttles.

This snowflake is made in 3 rounds, but do not cut the thread between the rounds.

Round 1: rings with 6 dk and 3 p. The last ring is made as a split ring.

Round 2: chains with 4 dk and 2 small p. There are also small picots between the chains.

Round 3: made up of rings and chains according to the diagram.

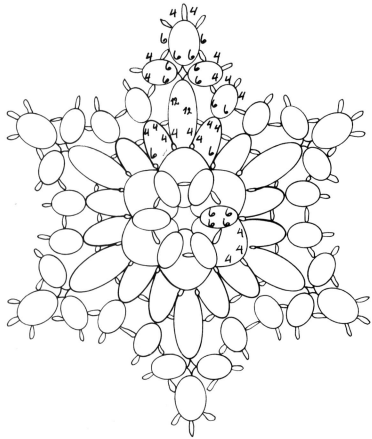

The Fifteenth Day of December

2 shuttles.
The snowflake is made in 2 rounds according to the diagram. The last picot in the inner ring is made as a false picot (see page 5).

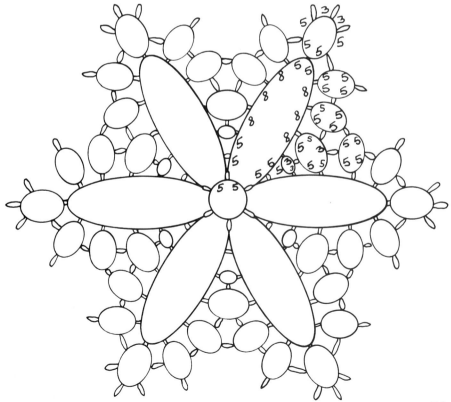

The Sixteenth Day of December

2 shuttles.
The snowflake is made continuously.
Start with the inner ring and make the last picot as a false picot (see page 5).
After this you start with a chain according to the diagram.

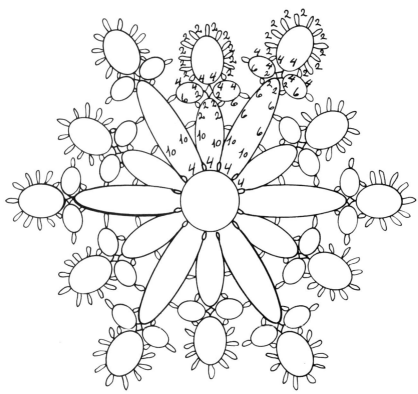

The Seventeenth Day of December

2 shuttles.
The snowflake is made in 2 rounds
according to the diagram.
There are 3 dk between each picot.
The rings A to G are made as split
rings.

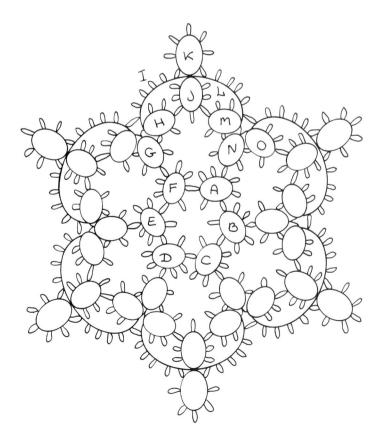

The Eighteenth Day of December

2 shuttles.
The snowflake is made in split rings according to the diagram.
There are 5 dk between each picot.

The Nineteenth Day of December

2 shuttles.
This snowflake is made continuously.
There are 6 dk between each picot.
Start with ring 1. Ring 2 and 3 are
split rings. Ring 4-6 and 5 are made
as ring on ring (see page 6).
DO NOT FORGET: Ring 16 has
to be joined to ring 3 before pulling
together.

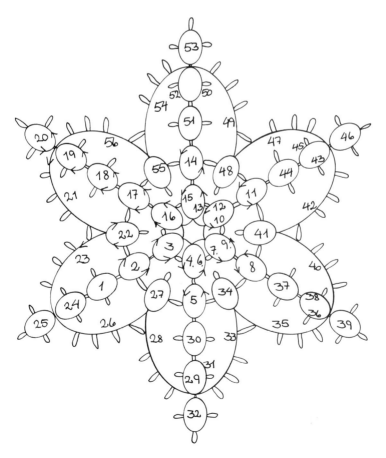

The Twentieth Day of December

Round 1: 1 shuttle + a ball thread.
Round 2: 2 shuttles.
The snowflake is made in 2 rounds according to the diagram.
By using a false chain between round 1 and 2 (see page 8 and 6) the snowflake can be made continuously.
There are 3 dk. between each picot.

The Twentyfirst Day of December

2 shuttles.

The snowflake is made in 3 rounds, but do not cut the thread between the rounds.

Josephine knot = 10 hk.

Round 1: start with a Josephine knot, then a normal ring. The last ring is a split ring.

Round 2: start with a split ring and proceed according to the diagram.

Round 3: start with a chain according to the diagram.

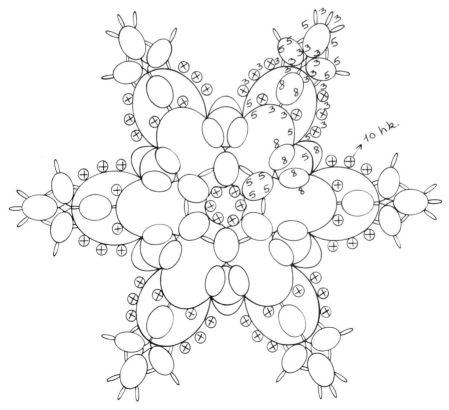

The Twentysecond Day of December

2 shuttles.

The snowflake is made in 2 rounds continuously.

Round 1: start with the ring in the middle. The chains are spirals consisting of 100 hk. Tat the ring on the top. Before you start the ring, make a small picot for joining round 2.

Round 2: consists of chains, tat according to the diagram.

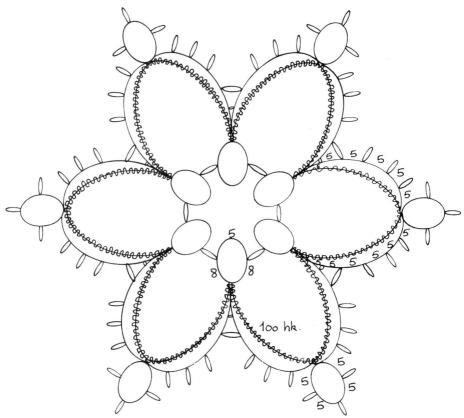

The Twentythird Day of December

Round 1: 1 shuttle + a ball thread.
Round 2: 2 shuttles.
The snowflake is made in 2 rounds according to the diagram.
The chains are spirals. When you join round 2 to round 1, crochet around all of the chain, no picot is made.

The Twentyfourth Day of December

2 shuttles + 18 glass beads 3mm in diameter.

The snowflake is made in 3 rounds.

Round 1: start with the ring in the middle (make 5 p, the 6th p is created when round 2 starts).

Round 2: start with a split ring, pull it together and make a small picot before you start the chain (the picot is for joining in in the next round). The chain is a spiral made of 75 hk.

Round 3: start with a split ring, then a chain according to the diagram.

Here glass beads are attached to the outer picots, but you can change this to your own liking.

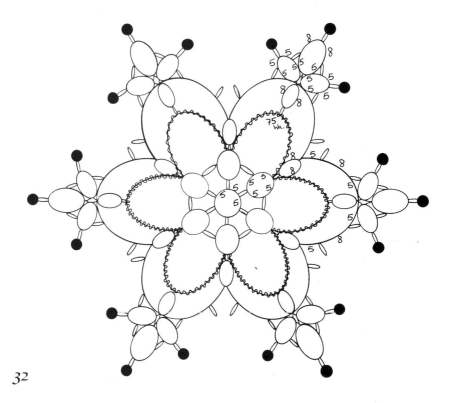